Art!
How Do I Start?

by

Chandrika Sanwal

MW00934495

To the girl who brings color, creativity, and curiosity to my life ...

Mumma

This Book Belongs To

_____

My name is Bart. The one thing I love most is art.

There's only one problem. I never know how to start!

Should I go to the local mart, pick supplies, and fill up a basket or cart?

Maybe I should just use scrap paper and scissors at home. Is that the best way to start?

I could make a chart. That would make me
feel extra cool and smart!

Should I draw a go-kart? I could attempt a
3D one with wheels so it could dart!

Ooh, I know! I could take a lemon apart and make a tart.

Hey, does anybody know if sour foods make you fart? (Oops!)

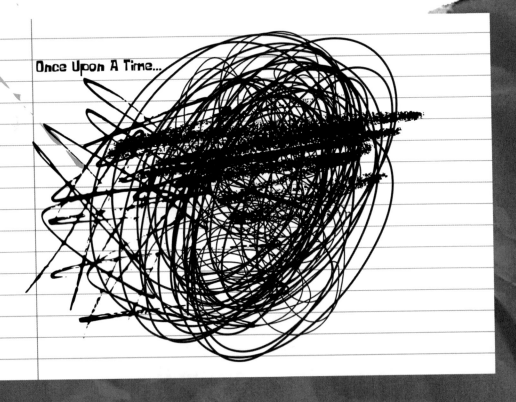

I could write and illustrate a story! It feels frustrating, though, when I mess up and have to restart.

Let's take a break to check out my friend's clay work. Do you like it as much as I do? Which part?

I'm learning how to play the French horn. I can play some notes for you before I depart.

Wow, there are so many forms of art! I guess this was my information to impart!

So ... how do I start?
Well, I think the answer is, and my friends
would agree:
"Express whatever is in your heart."

Time to get artsy (fartsy?)!

What art is in your heart?

About

the Author

Chandrika here! Former IT/Business Analyst and Project Manager, turned Full-Time Mom, turned Substitute Teacher, turning novice Children's Book Author. Phew! A Midwesterner at heart, I love getting to know everyone's story (while chomping on cheese). I am proud of both my Indian and American upbringing! I am a self-proclaimed word nerd and enjoy silly, light-hearted, clever humor. My passions include music, kids, travel, food, & coffee!

Made in the USA
Middletown, DE
04 December 2023

44369953R00015